SUMMER HAIKU

SUMMER HAIKU

OWEN BULLOCK

RECENT
WORK
PRESS

Summer Haiku
Recent Work Press
Canberra, Australia

Copyright © Owen Bullock, 2019

ISBN: 9780648404279 (paperback)

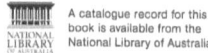

A catalogue record for this book is available from the National Library of Australia

All rights reserved. This book is copyright. Except for private study, research, criticism or reviews as permitted under the Copyright Act, no part of this book may be reproduced, stored in a retrieval system, or transmitted in any form by any means without prior written permission. Enquiries should be addressed to the publisher.

Cover image: © Dianne Firth 2017, *Canberra Tales III*, textile 42cm x 42cm, photographed by Andrew Sikorski

Dr Dianne Firth is Adjunct Associate Professor with the Centre for Creative and Cultural Research at the University of Canberra. Her layered and stitched textiles are informed by her training as a landscape architect. Firth's art work is recognised nationally and internationally through major exhibitions and public collections.

Cover design by Recent Work Press
Set by Jasmine Braybrooks

recentworkpress.com

Summer Haiku

summer heat
the snap and crack
of broom seeds

camp kitchen
a baby cockabully
in the rinsing bowl

fifth night camping
we find
the pillows

kayaking into dusk
below the bridge
the changing lights

often
as we get older
tears in our eyes

as she counts his toes
he mouths
the numbers

Christmas Eve—
the neighbour comes round
to borrow some data

yellow butterfly
from piece of air
to piece of air

night sky
losing count
of the satellites

change of weather
his umbrella becomes
a parasol

clinging
a plastic bag
in the ocean

farm tour
a llama cleans its teeth
on the fence wire

camp corn
the taste
of last night's smoke

teeth marks
in the soap
hedgehog-sized

50th birthday—
a bouquet of flowers
on the bridge

birthday walk
a goat carcass
beside the track

wind the trees gyrate

the river went
da da da da da all night long
the little girl says

an afternoon
without any wind ...
voices in the river

I would have given up
so many times ...
we mend the tent

frustration ...
a bull bellows
on the hillside

feeling only
its heat
hot flush

hawk dives
for the fifth time
nothing yet

not a man
but some kind of shadow—
daybreak

heat haze
grass ripples
up the slope

under water
the stream bed
peppered with leaves

eel bite
blood seeps out
the teeth marks

midday heat
a bumblebee
escapes the web

this time a finger ...
flash
of the white-bellied eel

i n c h w o r   m
finding its way
across the scrabble board

summer heat
a fly
rubs its legs together

hot pools
the arms
float

sunset

a rainbow crosses

horizons

bubbles in the stream
no more
than us

a bee
on a knife edge
walking

the river drops ...
I want to be impassive
as this stone

each time

you light the candle in the window

two candles

last sip
tasting it
for the first time

Winter Haiku

3pm

    ducks already folded

        into their bodies

young man
>	bouncing a rugby ball
>		as if it were round

outside in the frost
        whistling 'starry,
                starry night'

in your elf hat
>   looking up
>   'elfing'

ice covers the bucket—
      diving for the dipper
           in the night

over the collector's fire
gloves,
                five pairs of

she calls me cute
>   tears come easily
>>   this winter holiday

whispering
        so as not to disturb
           the stream

Kaitiakitanga—
> the river offers up
>> another boulder

gypsy wagon
      listening to a podcast
           about Derrida

the wagon steams
> in the frosty bowl

swaying here
      swaying there
            silhouettes of broom

with a torch
        afraid of what's beyond
                the ray of light

winter camping
        writing at the laundromat

scrabble
> putting down 'safe'
>> instead of 'self'

lying in bed

        light at the edge of fast-moving clouds

shallow bay at sunset
    the tide brings
        the colours in

Afterword

These haiku were written over three summers, camping on our piece of land near Waihi in Aotearoa New Zealand, and, for contrast, one winter sojourn there in our newly-built gypsy wagon. The land is bordered by the Mataura stream—which means 'red face'. We call the place 'Land of the shining stream' or 'River's edge'. The eels are named Brad and Angelina. One day, we'll build a house there. In the meantime, we're developing the land along permaculture principles, and noting moments both practical and transcendant.

Notes

Kaitiakitanga—the Maōri concept of guardianship of the land.

Derrida—Jacques Derrida, French philosopher best-known for his work on language and poststructuralism.

Acknowledgements

Some of these haiku previously appeared in *Kokako, Presence, Wales Haiku Journal* and *World Haiku Review.*

'I would have given up' won 2nd Prize in the Betty Drevniok Award, Haiku Canada, 2016.

'often' received a Merit Award in the World Haiku Review Vanguard section, August 2017.

'I would have given up' was reprinted in *Dust Devils: The Red Moon Anthology of English-Language Haiku 2016*, edited by Jim Kacian, et al.

'Christmas Eve' was reprinted in *A Hole in the Sky: The Red Moon Anthology of English-Language Haiku 2018*, edited by Jim Kacian, et al.

'I would have given up', 'Christmas Eve' and 'summer heat' appeared in the *Number Eight Wire: Fourth New Zealand Haiku Anthology*, 2019.

Thanks to Sue Peachey, Lucy Bullock, Toby Tuffery, Rose Tuffery, Caron Clay, Matt Morris, Shane Strange and Dianne Firth.

About the author

Owen Bullock is originally from Cornwall and lived for 25 years in Aotearoa New Zealand before migrating to Australia in 2014. He began writing haiku in 1999 and has published four collections: *Wild Camomile* (Post Pressed, 2009); *Breakfast with Epiphanies* (Oceanbooks, 2012); *Urban Haiku* (Recent Work Press, 2015), and *River's Edge* (Recent Work Press, 2016). He is a former editor of *Kokako*, New Zealand's only specialist haiku magazine, and was one of the editors who produced *Take Five: Best Contemporary Tanka, Vol IV* (Kei Books, 2012). He has also published three books of longer poems, *Sometimes the sky isn't big enough* (Steele Roberts, 2010); *Semi* (Puncher & Wattmann, 2017), and *Work & Play* (Recent Work Press, 2016), as well as the novella, *A Cornish Story* (Palores, 2010). Owen holds a PhD in Creative Writing from the University of Canberra where he currently teaches.

2019 Editions
Palace of Memory: An elegy **Paul Hetherington**
Acting Like a Girl **Sandra Renew**
A Coat of Ashes **Jackson**
Summer Haiku **Owen Bullock**
A Common Garment **Anita Patel**
Strange Stars: A Queer Poetry Anthology **Various**
Giant Steps **Various**
Some Sketchy Notes on Matter **Angela Gardner**
The Question Nest **Peter Bakowski**
Breathing in Stormy Seasons **Stephanie Green**
Strange Creatures **Alyson Miller**

2018 Editions
The Uncommon Feast **Eileen Chong**
Inlandia **KA Nelson**
Peripheral Vision **Martin Dolan**
The Love of the Sun **Matt Hetherington**
Moving Targets **Jen Webb**
Things I Have Thought to Tell You Since I Saw You Last **Penelope Layland**
The Many Uses of Mint **Ravi Shankar**
Abstractions **Various**
ACE: Arresting,Contemporary stories by Emerging Writers **Various**

all titles available from

www.recentworkpress.com

www.ingramcontent.com/pod-product-compliance
Lightning Source LLC
Chambersburg PA
CBHW032050290426
44110CB00012B/1025